T0150405

THE JAGUAR STORY

▲ The XK8 coupe in 1996 with its famous namesakes (left to right), the fixed-head XK150, XK140 and XK120.

THE JAGUAR STORY

GILES CHAPMAN

The History Press

First published 2019

The History Press
The Mill, Brimscombe Port
Stroud, Gloucestershire, GL5 2QG
www.thehistorypress.co.uk

British Library Cataloguing in Publication Data.
A catalogue record for this book is available from the British Library.

ISBN 978 0 7509 8924 4

Typesetting and origination by The History Press
Printed in China

CONTENTS

Introduction | 6

1 William's Winning Combination | 8

2 Cost-Conscious Style | 16

3 Jaguar's Leaps to Greatness | 29

4 Winners on Road and Track | 40

5 E-Type and XJ6, True Game-Changers | 59

6 Feline Decline Despite the V12 and XJ-S | 74

7 The Miraculous Turnaround | 87

8 New Cars and Engines as Ford Takes Control | 97

9 From X-Type to XF, the Jaguar Magic is Recast | 109

10 Jaguar Land Rover, Making British Cars Great Again | 120

INTRODUCTION

Jaguar is not one of the been surrounded by my research foundation stones of materials, it soon became obvious automotive history. Its origins the Jaguar story has really been are surprisingly humble. It has, propelled by exceptional characters, however, one of the richest heritages Towering over them all is William of any great marque, one that bulges Lyons, Jaguar's founder and driving with wonderful cars, astonishing force, but the colleagues he inspired technical achievements, competition to greatness are just as vivid in their heroism and industrious tenacity. I'll influences, and so are the leaders be frank: trying to distil the entire privileged to follow in Lyons' giant Jaguar story, with great images, in footsteps. For Jaguar is a living a book of this size was never going legend, whose future is as genuinely to be easy. But in the months I've exciting as its fantastic story so far.

◄ Sir William and Lady Lyons at home with dogs and, er, cats in the form of a 1930s SS 1 and 1970s Jaguar XJ.

➤ Sir William Lyons, looking stern yet dapper, with his world-famous E-type, outside his Wappenbury Hall home.

1 WILLIAM'S WINNING COMBINATION

Was there anything in William Lyons' background to signify the great career that lay ahead? No doubt this gave succour to the engineering apprenticeship he was undertaking at Manchester's Crossley Motors and a city technical school.

Raised in Blackpool, William entered this world on 4 September 1901 to parents who knew hard graft well. However, a position at Crossley, which made cars, lorries and buses, was not for Lyons. At age 19 he His father, also William Lyons, was an Irish immigrant who ran a musical instrument shop, and his mother Minnie was from a mill-owning family. They were modestly well off at best, and sent their son to the nearby secondary Arnold School, where he was a diligent student. left the firm and began work as a salesman for Brown and Mallalieu, a Sunbeam garage in Blackpool. His grasp of consumer psyche probably received a tremendous boost as a result.

Tall, good-looking and softly spoken, the teenage Lyons was intrigued by anything mechanical, and when he was 18 he bought and tinkered with an old Sunbeam motorbike. With a salary of his own, Lyons could really indulge his love of motorbikes. He became friendly with a near-neighbour, William Walmsley, who was busy sprucing up ex-military First World War bikes for the civilian market. Part of this

▼ A young, motorbike-obsessed William Lyons astride a stripped-down Harley Davidson.

involved building sidecars and selling the combinations at a healthy profit. The elegant, torpedo-shaped form of Walmsley's 'Swallow' sidecar, with its full-width wheel disc, added unusual style to motorcycling: if you were taking a young lady out along the blustery Lancashire coast of the early 1920s, one of these sidecars for her to travel in, instead of riding pillion, would be an inducement. Indeed, young William Lyons bought one to attach to his latest steed, a Norton.

Lyons could see so much potential in the sidecars that he proposed he and Walmsley go into business together to make and sell them. Their fathers each put up a £500 bank guarantee and the Swallow Sidecar Company business was established

William Lyons' adept salesmanship was evident early on. Not only did he organise Swallow's own stand at the 1923 Cycle & Motor Cycle Show at London's Olympia, but he persuaded four bike manufacturers to include Swallow sidecars in their displays too.

▶ The stylish, torpedo-like profile of Swallow sidecars set them apart from utilitarian rivals.

on Lyons' twenty-first birthday. Lyons immediately drove the venture forward, convincing his older partner (Walmsley was 31) to find extra factory premises in Blackpool so they could increase production. With Walmsley ramping up output, Lyons tackled sales and marketing; a classic entrepreneur was emerging.

By 1926 the business grew so much that everything was centralised on a spacious new factory in Blackpool's Cocker Street. The company's staff organised the move over just forty-eight hours, using a single removals lorry and their thirty pairs of hands. Already, people who worked for Lyons, such as Harry Teather, were displaying extraordinary loyalty to this dynamic young fellow.

There was additional impetus behind the move. Williams Lyons realised sidecars would soon sink in popularity because, with the Austin Seven's launch in 1922, motor-car ownership was booming. Priced at just £122, the little Austin famously provided a real car in miniature with four cylinders, four wheels and four seats. As affordable personal transport, it clearly represented the future. Occupants were shielded from the weather, and it was manifestly far safer than a motorbike. Like all cars of the era, the Seven had a separate chassis, and Austin

▲ Left: The Austin Seven started to put Britain on four wheels but its basic specification cried out for enhancement.
Right: Swallow's first coach-built car body turned an Austin Seven into this natty, pint-sized roadster.

offered several different body styles. Yet Sevens were invariably black, upright, boxy and dull-looking. So in 1926 Lyons and Walmsley designed a dainty two-seater roadster body for the Austin Seven frame, made from lightweight aluminium, with a cowled radiator shell, gracefully tapered tail, flowing mudguards with running boards, and a raked-back, V-shaped windscreen. Lyons was conscious that a high female approval rating would fuel demand, and so the car featured a vivid two-tone paint job, which included painted wire wheels.

Introduced in May 1927, the Austin Seven Swallow was offered at £175, with a detachable hardtop £10 extra. The car predated the similarly conceived MG Midget. It was quickly joined by a Seven Swallow saloon, and soon the company was ordering Austin Seven chassis in batches of fifty. Lyons had cleverly tapped into motorists' desire to stand out from the crowd without spending a fortune. By the end of the year the company name had changed to the Swallow Sidecar & Coachbuilding Company, and London distributor Henlys was eager to market the cars to the bright young things of the 'Flapper' era.

The company was flourishing, but Blackpool was a long way from the heart of Britain's motor industry in the West Midlands. Ever thinking ahead, Lyons and Walmsley next decided they needed to head

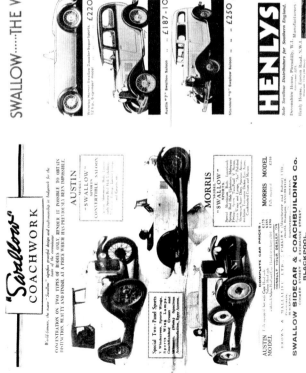

► Far left: this 1930 advert for Swallow coachwork includes both Austin and Morris cars.

◄ Left: London dealer Henlys helped market the many stylish models created by Swallow after its move to Coventry.

SWALLOW....THE WORLD'S MOST BEAUTIFUL COACHWORK

A big claim this, but who will say that it is not amply justified? Where else can you find such a brilliant range of bodies as those illustrated here . . . bodies of exquisite beauty and great strength . . . finished in a selection of no less than twelve artistically blended colour schemes; coachwork which enables you to express your individuality in a pleasing and unique manner.

But mere words are inadequate. You must see the full range of models now on view at Henlys, or write to-day for illustrated catalogue.

Wolseley Hornet Swallow 2-seater Super Sports. £220
12 h.p. 6-cylinder model

Austin "7" Swallow Saloon   ..   £187·10

Standard "9" Swallow Saloon   ..   £250

Swift "10" Swallow Saloon   ..   £269

HENLYS

Sole Stanliwp Distributors for Southern England.

Devonshire House, Piccadilly, W.1. Manufacturers: The Swallow Coachbuilding Co. Coventry

Henly House, Euston Road, N.W.1.

south if their business was really to prosper: it would cut costs and provide a greater pool of skilled labour. At the end of 1928, therefore, the whole operation decamped from Lancashire to Holbrook Lane, Foleshill, Coventry. The directors and many key staff members, Harry Teather included, made the move.

Although Swallow made its name with bespoke Austin Sevens, it offered coach-built bodywork for several other makes of cars, including Morris, Swift, Wolseley and even Fiat.

Once manufacture was up and running again, the partners' excellent organisational skills saw weekly output soar from twelve to fifty coach-built – yet affordable – cars. The 'house style' usually included a natty paint job (black over yellow was popular), a roofline profile as low as possible, and a stylish interior with pleasing touches like vanity mirrors. Fresh air was fed into the cabin via small, nautical-looking funnels ahead of the windscreen, trans-Atlantic liners being quite in vogue at the time.

Swallow had no trouble surviving the 1929 Wall Street Crash and resulting depression. Lyons appeared diffident in public, but in a 1977 TV interview he graciously accorded his company's early success to his workforce. 'I became impatient and felt it wasn't sufficient to build up a business on sidecars alone,' he recalled. 'The Austin Seven established the company on its feet. We had goodwill and enthusiasm from the workers. If we said we wanted to produce ten cars in a day then they would work until late at night until they were done. We had the right spirit. It was very good.'

2 COST-CONSCIOUS STYLE

After the trendy Swallow-bodied transformation had been executed on the Standard Big 9hp in 1929, the head of the Coventry carmaker John Black sensed an opportunity, and eagerly agreed to supply all the chassis Swallow needed. Meanwhile, Henlys' London salesmen were awestruck by a headline-grabbing new car from the USA, the powerful and long-bonneted Cord L-29. Could Lyons perhaps devise something British for them along similar lines?

Lyons, however, was even more ambitious. He was now determined to become a standalone carmaker, and John Black was happy to assist, especially after the widespread acclaim for

the rakish 1931 Swallow-bodied Standard 16hp. In early 1931 Standard agreed to supply Swallow with the 16's chassis racily modified: semi-elliptic leaf springs outside the members, a downswept centre section, lowered radiator, engine mounted 7in further back, and a 3in-extended wheelbase. Power units would be Standard's side-valve six-cylinder unit, in 2,054cc or 2,552cc sizes.

Henlys wanted to unveil the car at the London Motor Show at Olympia in October, but Swallow suffered a setback when the normally energetic William Lyons was rushed to hospital, where his appendix was removed. While recuperating, he discovered that Walmsley, in trying to marry the new car's desired

SS 1

On sale: 1932
Engine capacity, configuration:
2,054cc & 2,552cc,
straight-six-cylinder
Body style: two-door,
four-seater coupe
Dimensions: 4,420mm long,
1,397mm high, 1,524mm wide;
wheelbase: 3,023mm
Top speed: 70mph
Acceleration: 2,664cc (available
from 1934) – 0-60mph in 23sec.
Price: £310

look with the Standard chassis, had messed up. The cabin stuck up 'like a conning tower', raged Lyons. Walmsley's defence was that he had no choice, because otherwise no one of average height could have sat comfortably inside it.

It was too late to change it, but it didn't matter. The snug four-seater 'SS 1' at only £310 became an utter show-stealer. The company was quickly renamed once again, becoming the Swallow Coachbuilding Company (although sidecars continued to be made). What did SS stand for? Standard assumed it meant 'Standard Swallow', but Lyons chuckled: 'We called it the Swallow Special, the basis on which we decided to promote our own individuality.'

There were faults, such as leaky windscreen seals and a cockpit apt to fill with exhaust fumes. The 500 so the 1933 model (announced in style-conscious individuals who October 1932) received a complete rushed to order a SS 1 received a makeover, with lowered window and spritely cruiser rather than an out- door lines to match the bonnet, and and-out sports car.

Despite the rapturous reception, Lyons wanted the car dead right, mudguards that flowed through on

▼ The very first SS 1 of 1931, with its helmet-style mudguards and cabin that wasn't quite to William Lyons' liking.

to running boards. The chassis was redesigned and custom-manufactured by contractor Rubery Owen. It was now genuinely underslung at the back with members passing under the rear axle, so the cabin roofline could be lowered to Lyons' satisfaction. Together with a 7in wheelbase stretch, this meant two people could sit in the back in reasonable comfort.

The £325 cost was astonishing for a handmade two-plus-two. The two front bucket seats were beautifully leather-upholstered, while the inner door panels displayed the contemporary art deco motif of a rising sun, with a walnut centre and stitched leather 'rays'. There were twin picnic tables in the back.

This was a heavy car, with feeble Bendix cable-operated brakes. The alloy head on the '33 engine gave slightly better breathing, but 75mph (against 70 before) was the maximum speed. Customers, including film star George Formby, loved the car, perhaps fed by glowing press reviews such as this from *The Motor*: 'The SS 1 is a new type of automobile in the sense that it is a car built for the connoisseur but is relatively low priced. All the attributes of sports models are incorporated in a refined manner.'

Not every verdict was kind, though. Owners of expensive 'thoroughbred' cars were sniffy about the arriviste SS 1, with its lowly underpinnings. It was frequently dismissed as a 'cad's

An amazing performance

The Earl of Cardigan in the "Bystander" of Feb. 22nd, 1933, says—"I suppose that if one wanted to describe the S.S.1 in a mere half a dozen words, one would not go far wrong in calling it the most successful experiment in motoring. Why?... Because the S.S. is a combination of high-class coachwork of great beauty and supreme engineering achievement. Of 61 cars tested recently by the "Autocar," not one achieved the distinction of equalling the performance of the S.S.1 on speed, brake test and acceleration. The S.S.1 (16 h.p.) is the "thousand pound car" priced at £235. The S.S.II (9 h.p.) costs only £210.

Full details sent on request to Henlys Ltd., S.S. Southern England Distributors.

HENLYS
Henly House, 385/7 Euston Rd., N.W.1. Museum 7754 (20 lines)

► Henlys wanted a car with the long-bonneted look of America's Duesenberg, and Lyons was happy to oblige.

► The 1933-model SS 1 had a new, specially made chassis that allowed Lyons to get the low-slung, rakish lines he wanted.

car', 'spiv's Bentley', or 'Promenade sports car'. There was lingering resentment from the upper classes at the plurality of car ownership in the early '30s and this, from the *Daily Express* on 9 October 1931, probably fed their disdain: '"Dream" Car Unveiled, Designed by 22 salesmen': 'The salesmen were unanimous on one point: appearance is the best selling point in these days. "Give us a motor-car with a £1,000 look, but which costs £300, and life will be easy!"'

Swallow was burgeoning, yet a difference in philosophy was opening up between the partners. Walmsley was content to sit back and watch the money rolling in. He wanted a comfortable life and

the time to indulge his passion for model railways. The restless Lyons, however, sought to expand the company through ever-bolder moves. Their differing outlooks ultimately proved irreconcilable. Lyons bought Walmsley out in 1934, and almost immediately took his company public as SS Cars Limited.

To silence his detractors, Lyons wanted to build cars that needed no apology for their performance. Now he planned a new range of pukka SS cars to propel this step change. He employed consultant engineer Harry Weslake to redesign the cylinder head of Standard engines, to convert the side-valve unit to a more responsive overhead-valve configuration.

► This advert also includes the smaller SS II model; similar winning style but on a smaller Standard 9hp chassis.

►► Inside the Mayfair Hotel on 23 September 1935, where guests were open-mouthed at the low price asked for the new SS Jaguar saloon.

The beauty that is Swallow

Was beauty in car design ever before expressed in such striking fashion as it is in the 1935 S.S.I. Olympia will again emphasise that its individuality and distinction are beyond comparison.

A full four-seater Saloon with sliding roof, comprehensive and useful equipment, the S.S.I is a car to be desired by the motorist of discrimination. Luxurious interior, with quickly adjustable driver's

and front passenger's seats, and wonderfully comfortable "arm-chair" rear seats. Hand-buffed Hide upholstery tones with the extensive range of colour schemes. Price: 16 h.p. Model £325: 20 h.p. Model £10 extra. The S.S.II, embodying all those refinements usually associated with the most expensive models, now possesses four-speed gearbox. Price £210. Both models are exhibited on Stand 147, Olympia.

STAND 147 ▪️SS▪️ **OLYMPIA**

THE SWALLOW COACHBUILDING CO. LTD
FOLESHILL, COVENTRY. Coventry 8227

Manufacturers
Southern England Distributors:
HENLYS, DEVONSHIRE HOUSE,
PICCADILLY, W.1. Phone 7734 (20 lines)

In 2.5-litre form, power jumped from 70 to 104bhp, and Standard agreed to manufacture the units on SS's behalf. William Heynes joined the company to establish a proper engineering department.

Meanwhile, working with his coach-building manager Cyril Holland, Lyons created a sophisticated and expensive look for his new four-door SS saloon, whose proportions and detailing really did rival a handsome coach-built Bentley. Lyons chose the name Jaguar for his new 1.5-litre four-cylinder, and 2.5- and 3.5-litre six-cylinder saloon line-up.

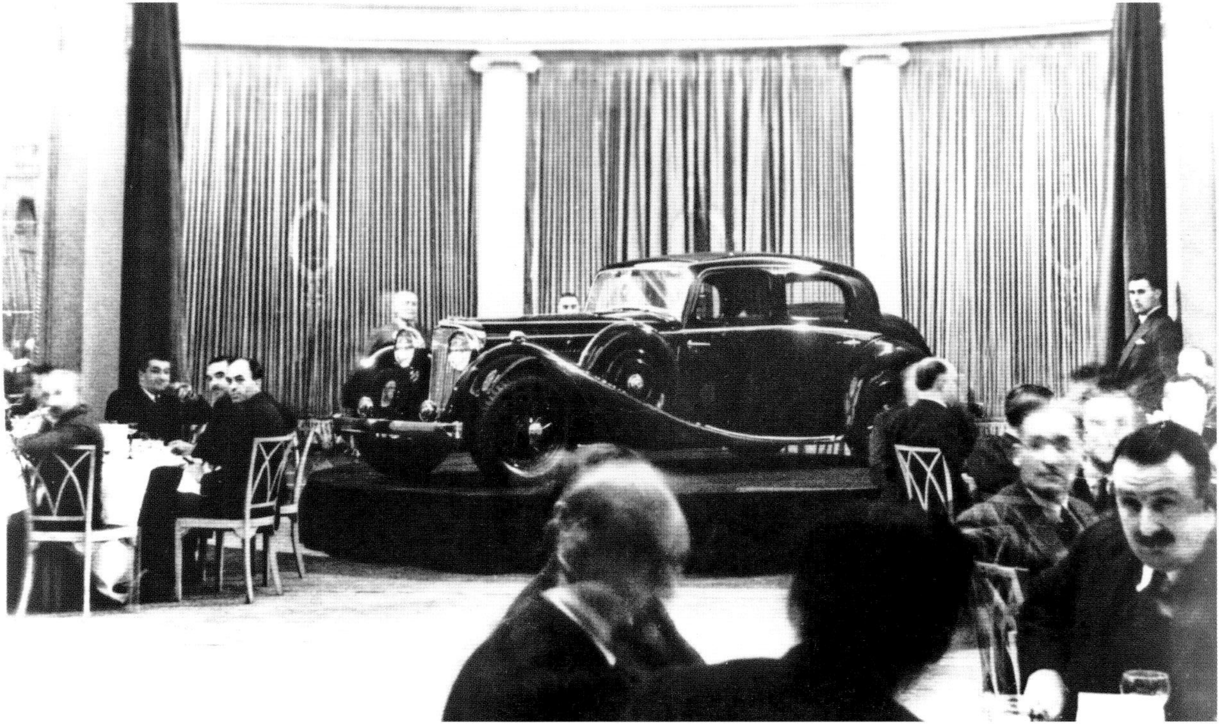

On 23 September 1935, at London's Mayfair Hotel, the cars were unveiled to astonished reporters and motor dealers. Over lunch, Lyons – he was just 33 – urged his guests to estimate the 2.5-litre SS Jaguar saloon's price. The average guess was £632, so there were gasps when Lyons revealed the list price as a paltry £395.

In 1936, Lyons pulled off another feat when he joined the world's sports-car maker ranks with his SS 100 Jaguar two-seater, following the very short-lived SS 90. It was the utter essence of the 1930s roadster with its short wheelbase, fold-flat windscreen, flowing mudguards and cutaway doors. What's more, it was lovely to drive, with an excellent gearbox, steering and brakes. It was a fast car with the 2.5-litre engine, capable of 95mph, but with the biggest 3.5-litre unit, available from 1938, its performance was electrifying – and it cost a bargain £445.

The SS 100 also put the company on the map in motor sport, after it contested and won numerous rallies including the RAC, Paris-Nice Trial, Alpine and Welsh events.

By 1938 SS was making fifty Jaguar saloons, drophead coupes and sports cars every day. A year later and annual output surpassed 5,000 cars, with ash-framed bodies replaced by all-pressed-steel construction to slash manufacturing costs and vehicle weight. But war

was looming, and the shrewdly run company (Lyons maintained his low prices were possible because SS was such a lean organisation) was ready for its part in Britain's military offensive.

▼ A sliding metal 'sunshine roof' on an SS Jaguar; a convertible 'drophead-coupe' body style was also offered.

SS 100 JAGUAR 3.5-LITRE

On sale: 1938–39
Engine capacity, configuration: 3,485cc, straight-six-cylinder
Body style: two-door, two-seater convertible
Dimensions: 3,886mm long, 1,272mm high, 1,600mm wide; wheelbase: 2,642mm
Top speed: 105mph
Acceleration: 0–60mph in 10.5sec.
Price: £445

▼▼ The SS 100 Jaguar is, for many, the acme of the 1930s roadster, a sports car that, with 3.5-litre engine, could reach 105mph.

▶ This SS 100
Coupe was exhibited
in 1938 but remained
a one-off; its design
clearly influenced
the later XK120.

Lyons tried to buy the bankrupt Sunbeam company from
the official receivers in 1935, to sell his new car range under
its name, but it was ultimately sold to the Rootes Group.
Instead, he chose the Jaguar name, after first seeking
permission to use it from Armstrong Siddeley, which made
an aero engine called a Jaguar.

SS started contributing to Meteor. The company's own design skills were used for experimental four-wheel drive vehicles for army dispatch messengers, although these were abandoned after the capacity of military transport planes increased massively.

War Department money was poured into the Foleshill infrastructure to fund this. Consequently, the company was strongly placed to restart car-making in 1945; the first new examples of the 1930s-style saloon car range (but sadly not the two-seater) left the production line in October. Not all its rivals were so fortunate: Triumph, for example, was wiped off the map after its factories were annihilated by German bombs.

SS started contributing to Britain's military defences even before the Second World War started in September 1939, producing wing components for Stirling bombers. By 1940, production of military trailers replaced Jaguar cars in the Holbrook Lane buildings. The *Luftwaffe* must have received excellent intelligence because six of the factory's shops were destroyed in Coventry bombing raids in 1940. However, they were soon up and running again, turning out Spitfire and Lancaster sections. SS then landed a valuable contract to repair and upgrade Armstrong Whitley bombers, and towards the end of the conflict it bagged another to build complete centre sections for the Gloster

One thing did need to change immediately: the company's name. The initials SS now had unfortunate connotations with the German SS paramilitary organisation, standing for *Schutzstaffel* and meaning 'Protection Squadron'. In March 1945, Lyons renamed his company Jaguar Cars Ltd.

Manufacturers were forced by the government to focus on exports to draw foreign currency to Britain and start to pay off the gigantic war debts it had necessarily sustained. To be allowed raw materials such as steel, companies had to demonstrate an export plan, and Jaguar did just that, sending off the first boatload of 'MkIV' cars to the USA in January 1947. Behind the scenes, though, William Lyons had

a masterplan, and it revolved around his long-held desire to build a luxury saloon that could attain the magic ton: 100mph.

No Standard engine, nor few others made in Britain, was anywhere near capable of powering such a car. But that wouldn't be a problem; Jaguar was about to introduce its very own.

During the darkest days of the war, while on fire watch together in the factory at night, William Heynes and engineers Claude Baily and Walter Hassan had drawn up plans for a fantastic power unit.

The straight-six-cylinder twin-cam masterpiece, uniting clever technical features with an engineering beauty of Bugatti's calibre to create a

▶▶ The XK120 as revealed to the world in 1948 as a rolling testbed for Jaguar's new XK engine.

▼ Details of the original XK120 including cockpit and boot space; most were exported and so were a rare sight in Britain.

flexible, powerful and tunable unit. It was an incredibly bold move as a first complete engine project, for no such engine had ever been mass-produced before, and Lyons backed it to the hilt.

Its basis was a cast-iron cylinder block with a seven-bearing crankshaft featuring steel con-rods. On top was placed an all-alloy cylinder head with hemispherical combustion chambers and a crossflow design, the work of consultant Harry Weslake. Twin overhead camshafts, two timing chains to reduce noise, and twin 1.75in SU carburettors completed the exotic specification.

The resulting 3,442cc engine produced 160bhp at 5,200rpm and

▲ At Jabbeke in Belgium in 1949, where the XK120 was proven to be capable of 132mph with its windscreen removed like this.

► BMW's 328 competing in the Mille Miglia in Italy in 1940. The 328 was a wonderful sports car that must have had an influence on the XK120.

with its polished aluminium cam covers and stove-enamelled exhaust manifold a matter of real pride for the owner.

As Jaguar was finding its feet again, development work continued apace on what was now called the XK engine. In 1948, with the new saloon's launch still two years away, Lyons pondered on how best to promote the XK, and decided at short notice to build a lightweight sports car as both a showcase for it and as a rolling testbed with which the company could start to gather the essential real-life experience of its performance and robustness.

The MkV saloon and drophead coupe were supposed to be Jaguar's big news at the first post-war London

had huge reserves of torque, yet was capable of being revved to high limits. It also proved to be uncommonly reliable. And once installed in cars, it looked superb,

Jaguar built its
first batch of
XK120s using
aluminium
panels, as
originally
intended, but the
main production
version was
re-engineered
with a steel body
to meet the huge
demand, and
that took more
than a year.

▲ To satisfy enormous demand, Jaguar rethought the XK120
production car, giving it a cheaper steel body.

➤ The gorgeous lines of the XK120 Coupe nonetheless made for quite a claustrophobic interior.

JAGUAR XK120 ROADSTER

On sale: 1948–54

Engine capacity, configuration: 3,442cc, straight-six-cylinder

Body style: two-door, two-seater convertible

Dimensions: 4,420mm long; 1,334mm high, 1,562mm wide; wheelbase: 2,591mm

Top speed: 120mph

Acceleration: 0–60mph in 10sec.

Price: £1,263

motor show in 1948. They featured a brand-new torsion-bar independent front suspension system, all-new chassis, updated engines and a delightful evolution of pre-war styling.

But Lyons now decided to exhibit his sports car at Earls Court too, naming it the XK120 in expectation of its potential top speed, and with a vague plan that he'd build a limited run of 240 cars, mainly intended to gain publicity through motor sport. William Lyons swiftly designed a sports-car body on a shortened MkV chassis, and had it beaten in aluminium in two months.

The tumultuous reaction to the XK120 took Lyons and everyone at Jaguar by total surprise. Its truly breathtaking lines mixed themes from the one-off SS 100 Coupe, BMW's 1940 328 Mille Miglia sports-racing car, and the very latest from Italian and French coachbuilders. It was beautifully, classically proportioned, and even today rates as a timeless shape. Thousands of people, unsurprisingly, wanted to place orders for the star of the show. Jaguar had gained all the publicity it could possibly have wished for.

Jaguar used a stretch of famously arrow-straight road at Jabbeke in Belgium to prove the XK120 could hit 120mph. Chief test driver Ron 'Soapy' Sutton drove one with hood raised and achieved a timed mile at 126.5mph, and over 132mph with windscreen and hood removed. This made it officially the world's fastest production car.

▲ One of Jaguar's fearless test drivers Norman Dewis at Jabbeke in October 1953, where this bubble-topped XK120 set an astonishing 132mph speed record.

▼▼ Jaguar dealer, and Lyons' son-in-law, Ian Appleyard tasted Alpine Rally victory in his famous 'NUB 120' XK120 roadster.

4 WINNERS ON ROAD AND TRACK

The XK120 was an absolute sensation, and once full-scale production was underway it took Jaguar into the most coveted global market of all: America's west coast. Teenage car-spotters in Britain almost never saw an XK120 splashing through the drizzle at home because they were nearly all exported!

At the London motor show in 1950, though, William Lyons' long-term dream was made real with the launch of the Jaguar MkVII. It couldn't be called the MkVI because Bentley already used that name, but this large, sweepingly stylish luxury saloon was so much more exciting than the Bentley anyway, with its 3.4-litre XK twin-cam engine. At 16ft long, it was huge by European standards,

but the powerful engine and excellent handling from the MkV-style chassis with independent front suspension, seemed to shrink its proportions to those of a nimble sports car once on the move; cornering and roadholding were extraordinary for a saloon of this bulk. In 1952 *The Motor* magazine **found that** this 2-ton machine genuinely was a 100mph car (they discovered its top speed was actually 101mph), while its performance was proven by five straight wins in Silverstone's production touring car race from 1952-56 – two of them down to Stirling Moss, and another to Ian Appleyard. In 1956, too, a high-performance MkVIIM won the Monte Carlo rally outright driven by a team headed by Ronnie Adams.

▲ All smiles as a Jaguar MkVII performs the opening duties at the Motor Industry Research Association proving ground at Nuneaton in 1954.

Moss and Appleyard were busy elsewhere helping to cement Jaguar's high-performance reputation. After the arrival of the svelte XK120 fixed-head coupe in 1951, William Heynes' personal example was taken to the Montlhéry Autodrome circuit near Paris, where Moss and three others drove it non-stop for seven days and nights at an average 100mph. No other car had ever achieved that. Appleyard, meanwhile, won the Alpine Rally three times in a row in his distinctive white XK120 registered NUB 120, 1950–52. His co-driver was his wife Pat, who happened to be William Lyons' daughter.

With expansion on every front, Jaguar outgrew its Holbrook Lane home, even after 13 acres of adjacent

▶ Left: Stirling Moss at Le Mans in 1951 in the Jaguar C-type in which he set a new course lap record.

Right: the Rolt/Hamilton C-type on its way to Jaguar's second Le Mans 24-hour victory in 1953.

William Lyons was knighted for his services to British exports in the New Year Honours list in 1956, and Sir William was proud to give the Queen and the technology-obsessed Duke of Edinburgh a tour of the bustling Browns Lane plant that April.

land had been acquired and built on. Lyons identified a site in the western Coventry suburb of Allesley, the 'Number Two Shadow Factory' built by the government in the late 1930s to produce tank engines, and now standing idle. The factory in Browns Lane, was ideal, and offered 1 million sq ft of manufacturing space. Lyons bought it in a deal with Sir Archibald Rowland of the Ministry of Supply, on condition Jaguar continued to make Meteor tank engines there. Starting in May 1951, an entire department – the machine shop first, the paint shop last – moved in each weekend, with the colossal undertaking complete on 28 November.

At Browns Lane, Jaguar's fledgling Competitions Department could now expand, under the experienced eye of service manager Frank 'Lofty' England, a former race-team manager. Its key objective was to take the XK120 to the pinnacle of motorsport success – a win in the punishing Le Mans 24-hour race – and to that end Jaguar developed a bespoke racing version, the XK120C (for Competition) or 'C-type', that transplanted the XK engine – tuned to 204bhp – into a spaceframe chassis, with a new body designed by former Bristol Aeroplane Company aerodynamics guru Malcolm Sayer. Chief engineer William Heynes oversaw the project, with Lyons' uppermost concern being that any pure racing Jaguar should not disgrace itself in public.

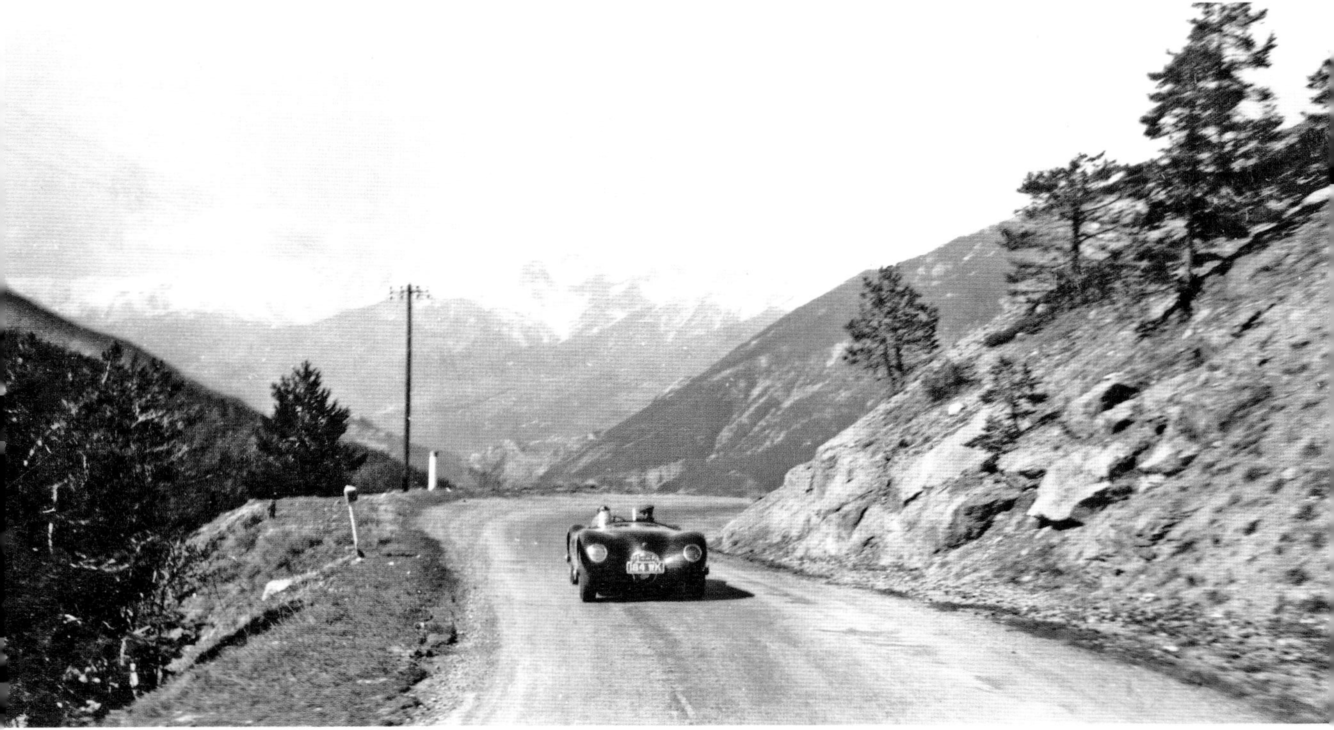

It was a measure of how professional the company was in everything it now did that the C-type thundered to a stunning victory in the 1951 Le Mans race, driven by Peter Walker and Peter Whitehead. The feat was repeated in 1953 with drivers Tony Rolt and Duncan Hamilton, and an important technical innovation gave Jaguar a unique edge on rivals – the pioneering fitment of Dunlop disc brakes, developed from aircraft systems and resistant to the dreaded brake fade. It was, in fact, a C-type walkover: the cars finished second and fourth overall too.

And nor was Jaguar's dominance of the French day-and-night endurance race over. It was back

with an all-new car in 1954, the semi-monocoque D-type with its characteristic wind-cheating stabilising fin flowing out from behind the driver's headrest. With all-round disc brakes and capable of 179mph, it could accelerate from 0 to 60mph in a blistering 4.7sec. Pipped to the winning post by a Ferrari by under two minutes in '54, the D-type achieved a hat-trick of Le Mans triumphs in 1955 (Mike Hawthorn/Ivor Bueb), 1956 (Ron Flockhart/Ninian Sanderson) and 1957 (Flockhart/Bueb). After that, Jaguar withdrew from motor racing – what more was there to prove?

Competition provided the glamour and headlines, but Jaguar's production car line-up was

▼◀ A Jaguar C-type taking part in the 1953 Mille Miglia (1,000 Miles) road race in Italy.

▶ Tony Rolt in the first D-type number XKD401 before the 1954 Le Mans race, with William Lyons just behind him.

continually evolving. A drophead coupe joined the XK120 roadster and coupe in 1953, and a year later the whole range became the XK140 series, with rack and pinion steering and a roomier cabin for the luxurious closed car. By the time the XK150 series arrived in 1958, they'd become refined grand tourers rather than hardcore sports cars. Meanwhile, the MkVII became the MkVIII in 1954, gaining Jaguar's first automatic gearbox and a styling makeover that included two-tone paintwork. When the car became the MkIX in 1958 it offered all-round disc brakes and power-assisted steering.

Jaguar invested £1 million in a brand-new compact model, the 2.4-litre, unveiled in 1955. It was

▼ A D-type with key Jaguar people, left to right: Malcolm Sayer, William Heynes, Bob Knight, test driver Ron 'Soapy' Sutton, engineers Arthur Ramsay and Keith Cambage, and (seated in the car) Norman Dewis.

▶ A Jaguar D-type taking the chequered flag at Le Mans in 1957, with Ron Flockhart at the wheel.

the first sports saloon as we know them today, and broke new ground for the company in adopting chassis-free unitary construction. The engine was a smaller version of the well-proven XK, and its fairly lacklustre performance was fixed when a 120mph 3.4-litre stablemate joined it in 1957. This one certainly did benefit from the disc brakes added a year afterwards, because it had developed a rather hairy reputation that needed fixing. 'The car seldom did anything frightening, but I often had the feeling it might,' wrote Lord Montagu, while the car-mad MP Alan Clark recorded: 'The 3.4 MkI, that really was a car; it didn't have any brakes at all.'

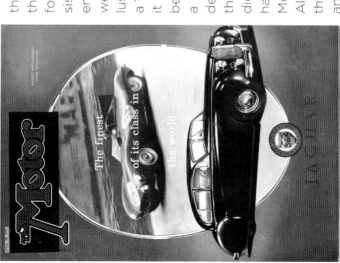

▼ Jaguar harnessed its race track success to help promote its road-going cars, as in this 1955 *The Motor* magazine cover advert.

▲ Jaguar's D-type used British science and stamina to take the sports-car-racing battle to Italy's Ferrari.

▼▼ A tail fin added to later D-types to aid their high-speed stability was also a very distinctive statement of Jaguar's intent.

Just one year later, these cars were rendered 'Mk1s' when the Mk2 series arrived. The remarkable revamp they received, overseen by William Lyons, had a similar effect to his early revision of the SS 1; his expert eye bestowed the cars with a subtle facelift and enlarged windows, keeping them fresh and desirable throughout the 1960s, while a wider rear track and redesigned rear suspension tamed the wayward handling. A 220bhp 3.8-litre engine option created a 125mph version that was a spectacular performer in saloon-car racing, and also the best getaway car any bank robber could want ...

▶ Left: Ivor Bueb zooming to 24-hour endurance victory in the Jaguar D-type, entered by the Ecurie Ecosse team at Le Mans in 1957.

Right: among the benefits of the 1954 XK140, which replaced the 120, was a more spacious and comfortable cabin for the coupe.

In 1957 Jaguar announced a roadgoing edition of the D-type racer, the XKSS, but just sixteen of them were built before a factory fire destroyed the production jigs (and 270 other cars). This wasn't before Hollywood petrolhead Steve McQueen had bought one – he kept it for ten years, and its high speeds brought him two driving bans.

JAGUAR MK2 3.8-LITRE

On sale: 1959–67

Engine capacity, configuration: 3,781cc, straight-six-cylinder

Body style: four-door, five-seater saloon

Dimensions: 4,591mm long, 1,432mm high, 1,695mm wide; wheelbase: 2,730mm

Top speed: 125mph

Acceleration: 0–60mph in 8.5sec.

Price: £1,779

▶ Jaguar's lovely XK150 roadster, one of the first sports cars in the world to feature four-wheel disc brakes.

▲ A bustling scene at the Browns Lane plant in c.1962, with Mk2 and MkX saloons nearing completion.

▲ The MkIX of 1958 offered standard two-tone paintwork and power steering as part of its luxury package.

▼ The 1955 2.4-litre used Jaguar's first unitary-construction (not needing a separate chassis) hull.

▸ The 3.4-litre saloon of 1957 was powerful enough to go saloon-car racing but cried out for better brakes at first.

▲ With deft updates to its chassis and styling, the Mk2 came to embody the 1960s compact sports saloon.

▲ Once criminals realised what a good getaway car the Mk2 made, the police had to follow suit, as shown in this evocative magazine cover.

▶ The D-type-based XKSS, beloved of Steve McQueen, had its prospects cut short by a devastating factory fire in 1957.

5 TRUE GAME-CHANGERS

E-TYPE AND XJ6,

The impact of the Jaguar E-type's unveiling at the 1961 Geneva motor show was huge. It emerged from a large wooden packing case into a frenzy of flashbulbs. An instant must-have, its aggressive, dart-like profile, with a lengthy, bulging bonnet and tapering, pointed tail were like nothing else on the road.

Jaguar's streamlining expert Malcolm Sayer had taken the purposeful contours of the D-type racer and made sure they worked for a road car, while adding necessities like bumpers and a proper hood

(and even a practical hatchback third door on the coupe). Here, the gifted yet untrained stylist William Lyons' unerring eye for detail had, as ever, been invaluable. A front number plate would have ruined looks and aerodynamics, so owners were obliged to have one as a sticker on the bonnet.

The E-type was the result of four years' work at Jaguar, an unparalleled project to capitalise on all that the company had learnt from high-speed endurance motor racing and package it into a road car that could hit Lyons' next target – 150mph.

The basic design layout followed D-type thinking, a torsionally strong monocoque main body tub with a bolted-on front subframe cradling a 3.8-litre XK engine and the front suspension. The suspension itself was one of the car's star features: it was the work of chief development engineer Bob Knight, independent all-round with double wishbones at the front and a wishbone/coil spring set-up at the back. It gave the E-type its superb amalgam of sporty roadholding and excellent ride comfort. Knight reportedly completed the design in twenty-seven days, to win a £5 bet from Lyons that it couldn't be done in a month.

Jaguar knew it had the makings of a motoring icon even then; it could leave nothing to chance. Demonstration cars loaned to magazines offered blistering performance, with the roadster hitting 149mph and the magic 150mph for the coupe. But those cars, it later emerged, were cunningly doctored: any E-type owner trying

JAGUAR E-TYPE SERIES I 4.2-LITRE COUPE

On sale: 1964–68
Engine capacity, configuration: 4,235cc, straight-six-cylinder
Body style: two-door, two-seater coupe
Dimensions: 4,458mm long, 1,225mm high, 1,653mm wide; wheelbase: 2,438mm
Top speed: 140mph
Acceleration: 0–60mph in 7sec.
Price: £2,097

to match these speeds – say on the 72-mile long M1 that opened in 1959 and had no upper speed limit until 1965 – found it impossible to bust the 140mph barrier ...

At its Geneva revelation, Jaguar took 500 orders; a month later in April 1961, the car was at the New York Auto Show, where six were sold

in the first half-hour. Frank Sinatra saw the car there and barked: 'I want that car and I want it now.' Even Enzo Ferrari proclaimed the E-type 'the most beautiful car ever built' on first sight.

As ever with a Jaguar, it was a steal: the E-type roadster was £2,097. A Mercedes-Benz 300SL

▲ Left: profile of an all-time great; even Enzo Ferrari declared the E-type the most beautiful car he'd ever seen.

Right: Sir William Lyons introducing his E-type fastback coupe to astounded reporters at Geneva in 1961.

► E-type roadsters lined up at the Browns Lane factory, awaiting mass collection by their lucky owners.

contrast, a small family car like the Triumph Herald cost £708, and an average house about £2,700.

It was never intended for competition but an E-type won the first race it entered, with Graham Hill driving at Oulton Park. Jaguar never totally deserted the tracks; in 1963 it built a few special lightweight E-types constructed almost entirely of aluminium that achieved several race victories in the USA.

Incredibly, the E-type wasn't the only striking new Jaguar of 1961. There was also the large and mightily impressive MkX executive saloon, true chairman transport and with its huge size intended to attract wealthy US buyers. Gone was the separate chassis of the venerable

roadster cost £5,698, an Aston Martin DB4 £4,084, while a Ferrari 250GT was megabucks at £6,469, and a Bentley SII Continental positively unattainable at £9,115. By

MkIX, replaced by full monocoque construction. There was all-round independent suspension, power steering and most were sold with automatic transmission. Initially Jaguar landed £25m-worth of orders from the USA and Canada, although enthusiasm for the car soon waned, and it struggled a little as the decade wore on. Jaguar found more success with the 1963 S-type and 1966 420, both developments of the more compact Mk2 with E-type-style independent rear suspension, more graceful styling and 3.8- and 4.2-litre versions of the XK engine respectively.

There was also a 420 doppelganger, named the Daimler Sovereign but otherwise near-identical.

In 1966 Jaguar built a dramatic mid-engined sports car planned to return the company to racing. The so-called XJ13 was intended to use an all-new V12 power unit, but it was axed after Jaguar became part of British Leyland. Although the prototype was wrecked in a crash in 1971, it was subsequently rebuilt and is in fine form today.

Getaway people
get Super National

Pale sunrise and purple evening ... getaway, getaway hours! Sleek, beckoning roads and away, from it places ... getaway playgrounds! This is your moment. Relish the power of Super National. Getaway people get Super National.

GETAWAY PEOPLE
GET SUPER NATIONAL

National

▶ 1960s car culture embraced the E-type, as seen here in an advert for National petrol and on a teenagers' annual featuring owner Tony Blackburn, the DJ who opened Radio 1 in 1967.

Jaguar acquired Daimler in 1960 for its extensive Coventry factory space, and from now on a Daimler edition of Jaguar's saloons was generally offered.

A 4.2-litre engine also arrived in the Series II E-type in 1964. It offered much more torque, and also came with an improved gearbox (designed and built in-house and thankfully now featuring synchromesh on first gear), and a revised cockpit that sported much more comfortable seats. A couple of years later the E-type also gained a 2+2 seating option, with a somewhat ungainly taller roof, for the eager driver with speed-loving toddlers.

As the 1960s wore on, and Jaguar grew further, William Lyons was increasingly twitchy about the

▼ One of the rare, all-aluminium E-type Lightweights competing at Silverstone in 1963.

▼ This Jaguar 420G, the later, retitled version of the MkX, was Sir William Lyons' own example, photographed at his former home, Wappenbury Hall, Leamington Spa.

future. As a relatively small car manufacturer, he worried about survival, and Jaguar's ability to keep being resourceful while also relying on outside suppliers. His fears were confirmed when the firm stamping Jaguar's car bodies, Pressed Steel Fisher, was acquired by the British Motor Corporation in 1965. This forced him to pursue a merger with BMC, maker of the Mini and MG sports cars, and in 1966 Jaguar and BMC united to become British Motor Holdings (BMH).

Just two years later, the British motor industry regrouped again, under pressure from politicians in Whitehall. BMH and Leyland Motors merged to form British Leyland Motor Corporation.

That same year, Jaguar's sprawling array of saloon cars – 240/340 (formerly Mk2), S-type, 420 and 420G (a renamed MkX) – was replaced in one fell swoop by a single, exceptional new model: the XJ6. At the time, and for years afterwards, the XJ6 was widely regarded as the finest saloon car on sale. Thanks to Bob Knight's painstaking work on development, the XJ set new standards of noise, vibration and harshness suppression, while its anti-dive suspension geometry and wide, specially designed Dunlop radial tyres produced an astounding combination of incisive road manners and soft, restful ride quality.

Jaguar historian Andrew Whyte gave an insight into Knight's

approach: 'The idea that development towards the ultimate should ever stop is anathema to Bob Knight. He never failed to use every last available moment to perfect some detail.' This was fully evident in the XJ6.

There were 2.8- and 4.2-litre versions of the XK engine, and the wonderfully sleek, tapered profile and broad, flat bonnet was again proof of Lyons' intuitive feel for automotive design. The driving position and all-round visibility from

► The sumptuous interior of the MkX was everything a successful captain of industry could wish for.

▲ Building up the structure of an E-type (a Series III coupe) at Browns Lane, with welding still done by hand.

the cosseting cabin were exemplary. Prices, as ever, were remarkable. The 4.2 cost £2,253, against £6,795 demanded for a Mercedes-Benz 300SEL. It was considered so instantly recognisable as a Jaguar that the marque name featured nowhere on the car itself, and William Lyons appeared in person in the advertising campaign to present the car to an eager public.

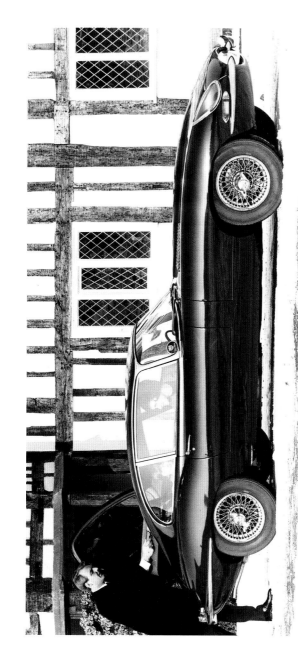

▲ A two-plus-two E-type joined the line-up in 1966, sacrificing a little purity of line for family-friendly practicality.

▲ Police forces across Britain ordered the powerful S-type as a high-performance pursuit car for their fleets.

▲ Probably the most famous small-screen Jaguar of all was this Mk2 featured in ITV's *Inspector Morse*, played by John Thaw.

▼ The sole XJ13 prototype, with its mid-mounted V12 engine, was rebuilt for posterity after being wrecked in 1971.

Clockwise from top left: the last of the Mk2 line was the 240 of 1967 kept competitively priced with simpler bumpers and vinyl upholstery; a prototype Jaguar XJ6 undergoing punishing testing while thinly disguised to evade identification; the original XJ6 was another massive hit for Jaguar – its compromise between sporty handling and cosseting ride comfort was unparalleled.

▶ Queen Elizabeth II and Prince Philip using a specially modified XJ6 on an official visit to Mauritius in 1972.

6 FELINE DECLINE DESPITE THE V12 AND XJ-S

The XJ6 boded well for Jaguar in the 1970s. The Coventry marque's biggest problem had been tasked with making the 5-litre was working overtime to satisfy demand and reduce the constant waiting list. Nonetheless, this world-beating sports saloon (with a slightly more formal Daimler model added in 1969) wasn't quite the machine Lyons and his team intended to create.

For one thing, it was initially planned as a longer, saloon version of the E-type, with similar front and rear styling. That idea was wisely scratched early on from the car codenamed XJ4 (Experimental Jaguar No. 4) to confer the XJ6 with the individual identity it merited.

For another, engineering legends William Heynes and Claude Baily had been tasked with making the 5-litre quadruple-camshaft V12 engine from the XJ13 a facet no other super-saloon offered. That proved too complicated so, after Heynes and Baily had retired, Walter Hassan and Harry Mundy produced a simpler, single overhead-camshaft design, at a capacity of 5.3 litres. It was all-aluminium but schemed to be robust enough to enter mass-production - engines of a similar configuration from Ferrari and Lamborghini were essentially handmade.

All this thoughtful redesign work meant the engine missed the deadline to appear in the first XJ6.

▼ The XJ12 was launched in 1972 and overnight became the most desirable saloon car on the planet.

▶▶ A snug fit for the 5.3-litre Jaguar V12 engine perhaps, but then again, the car was actually designed around it.

One of William Lyons' personal favourite Jaguars was the two-door version of the XJ6/XJ12, known as the XJ-C, on sale between 1974 and 1977. Only 10,000 of these elegant pillarless coupes were built.

Instead, it made its public debut in 1971 in the E-type Series III, ousting the XK and featuring four SU carburettors, since a reliable fuel-injection system wasn't yet deemed ready. The V12 E-type was now convincingly a 150mph rocket – a welcome late-life fillip so this £3,343 beast could hold its own with other '70s 'supercars'.

A year later the engine finally arrived in the XJ, as the XJ12. With a top speed of 147mph, it was the fastest four-seater on the planet, and by far the most refined; a long-wheelbase version added injection limousine-like accommodation.

It was the crowning glory to everything that Sir William Lyons had achieved, trouncing rivals on every front. His retirement that year should have been laced with satisfaction. However, the prevailing atmosphere around all that he'd so brilliantly built from scratch was anything but celebratory.

The problem was its place within the increasingly fractured British Leyland. Bob Knight joined the Jaguar Cars board in 1969; after Lyons and

► In 1971, the E-type – this is the Series III roadster – became the first production car powered by Jaguar's amazing V12 engine.

▼ This 1974 XJ12L was to USA specification, one of the many cars bound for the crucial North American market.

JAGUAR XJ12 SERIES 1

On sale: 1972–73

Engine capacity, configuration: 5,343cc, V12

Body style: four-door, five-seater saloon

Dimensions: 4,814mm long, 1,343mm high, 1,768mm wide; wheelbase: 2,764mm

Top speed: 150mph

Acceleration: 0–60mph in 7.4sec.

Price: £3,726

Frank England left, Knight found himself virtually alone in defending Jaguar's modus operandi. He did everything in his power to resist having Jaguar's engineering base diluted by folding it into Rover or Triumph. Meanwhile, British Leyland seemed hell-bent on destroying the company's soul. Knight was accustomed to working on slender resources but via short chains of command to produce engineering alchemy. Now he proved an unlikely but effective street-fighter, doggedly holding together Jaguar's independent nucleus – its close-knit engineering and design teams, operating on absolute shoestrings – while British Leyland head office made such morale-wrecking moves as renaming the Browns Lane factory as 'Large Car Plant No. 2', in true Soviet style. Long-standing employees were dismayed; Jaguar loyalty was woven into the company – Harry Teather, for example, one of the very first Swallow employees in 1922, retired in 1972 when he was purchasing director.

➤ Left: one of the very last V12 E-type roadsters of 1975, this one featuring the rare factory-supplied hardtop.

Right: the two-door XJ, in this case a V12-powered XJ 5.3C, was known to be the one William Lyons liked best.

Despite the corporate turmoil, Jaguar still managed to cause a major stir with the 1975 launch of the XJ-S. It replaced the venerable E-type but was a very different car – a two-plus-two grand tourer with effortless, continent-shrinking performance from its V12 engine, now fitted with Lucas fuel injection.

Underpinning the XJ-S was the XJ saloon floorpan, but the shape of the car again reflected the close collaboration between the aesthete William Lyons and the scientist Malcolm Sayer. Still, its flat, broad bonnet, oval headlights, and the aerodynamic 'flying buttresses' above the rear wings proved controversial

at first. Air conditioning was included as standard, and it could accelerate from 0 to 60mph in 6.9sec. However, by the time the car appeared in the TV series *The New Avengers* and *Return of the Saint* in the late 1970s the buying public was fully on-side with Jaguar's new departure.

The latter half of the 1970s was an unhappy time for Jaguar, corralled with Rover and Triumph into one particularly uncohesive operating division. British Leyland was bankrupt by 1975 and nationalised by the Labour government. Jaguar, the epitome of entrepreneurial automotive spirit, was now in state ownership. In parallel with other parts of British Leyland, industrial relations at Jaguar – always very co-operative and productive under the uniting aegis of Lyons – took a nosedive, and build quality suffered, with warranty claims and customer restiveness snowballing. The XJ Series II models introduced in 1973, the 3.4-litre XJ6 of 1975, and even

the Daimlers expensively trimmed
by London coachbuilder Vanden
Plas, all picked up reputational
scars as a result. Between 1978 and
1980 Bob Knight (he was bestowed
with a CBE in 1977) was officially
managing director, but he couldn't

see off every stupid diktat from BL
head office, such as that XJ6 colour
choice be limited to just red, white
and a notably horrible yellow.

It seemed Jaguar was in terminal
decline. The fact that Mk2s were
now valueless used cars, frequently

smashed to bits in banger races, was almost a sad metaphor for how far this former jewel in the crown of British car-making had fallen. As marques like BMW, Saab, Volvo and Audi broadened the choice of the prestige car market, Jaguar seemed to be fading fast.

▶ This glorious 1977 XJ-S carries an insignia on its door celebrating the Queen's Silver Jubilee of that year.

The Series III XJ range was introduced in 1979, with a newly designed roof and glazed area to improve rear headroom, and several other refreshed details. For the first time ever, the styling work was undertaken by an external consultant, in this case the Italian company Pininfarina.

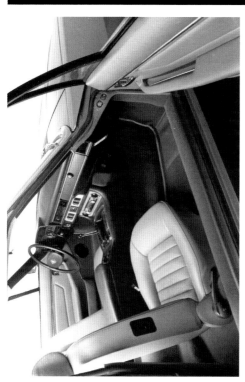

▲ Wide doors opened on to the XJ-S's opulent interior, with small rear seats behind the two supportive armchairs upfront.

▼◀ The most controversial aspect of the XJ-S was its characteristic 'flying buttresses' atop the rear wings, designed for high-speed stability.

Jaguar XJ-Ss featured in the late 1970s TV return of both *The Saint* (right) and *The Avengers* (above), the latter also featuring this special racing-style XJ 5.3C.

As the 1980s dawned there came a glimmer of hope in the gloom confronting Jaguar. The businessman tasked with 'rescuing' British Leyland, Michael Edwardes, had already given Land Rover its autonomy as a self-contained unit within the company and now he did the same for Jaguar Cars Ltd. This meant appointing a new chief executive, who arrived in April 1980 in the shape of dynamic former Unipart and Massey Ferguson manager John Egan, and promising him near-total autonomy. As Egan drove through the Browns Lane gates on his first morning, he found workers congregating to decide

on an all-out strike. Once inside, he encountered managing director Bob Knight, who promptly resigned.

'He must have thought I was just another agent of the devil, like the others,' Egan recalled recently.

The sales director Bob Berry buggered off too. Some of the old Jaguar people had been fighting this rearguard action for years. They just didn't think we'd make it. When I saw the Pininfarina-facelifted XJ6, I knew that car could sell... if we could just make it work. And the XJ-S! I presumed they were still building them, but they'd not made one for years. It had even more problems than the XJ6.

Egan attacked the company's quality problems like a man possessed. First, he negotiated the transfer of the Castle Bromwich body plant back from BL to total Jaguar control, and the quality of its basic shells soon improved hugely. Simultaneously, he led a programme to iron out the XJ6's myriad bugbears. Just making the windscreen and doors fit properly, Egan says, saved the loss-making Jaguar £20m. Fitting an extra cooling fan to the XJ6 – which BL had forbidden on cost grounds – cured the overheating that exasperated many owners. Parts suppliers were ordered to up their game or be replaced.

'Other British-made cars had faults too, so it wasn't unique, just a lot worse,' he said:

It would take dealers half a day to make the cars saleable, with twenty or thirty faults to fix. Everything was subject to quality and productivity improvements as we went along.

People had to work smarter. We did it with the enthusiasm and sup-port of the workforce. The shop stewards were telling them: you're crazy; follow us and we'll get you more money for doing less work. We were saying: you've got to put some effort into it. I wondered what people had been doing all these years. It was mystifying.

The man-hours needed to build an XJ6 fell from 700 to just 300.

Meanwhile, the XJ-S was resus-citated in 1981. A new of HE (High

Efficiency) cylinder head was designed and fitted, the work of specialist Swiss engineer Michael May, which reduced fuel consumption of the thirsty V12 engine by a fifth with little loss of power or torque. As well as enjoying vastly better build quality, the XJ-S HE received new alloy wheels and exterior decor, and burr walnut on its dashboard. The XJ-S was also chosen as the car to herald an all-new engine, known as the AJ6, in 1983. This straight-six 3.6-litre power unit was intended to replace the XK (although it didn't entirely, not for nine years) with a choice of head designs, the high-performance 24-valve iteration offering 225bhp. Because it featured an alloy block, the AJ6 weighed 30 per cent less

Jaguar's Bob Knight proved a cunning defender of the marque's core values. To thwart any British Leyland plans to cut corners on the XJ40, for example, he's said to have deliberately shaped the engine compartment so a Rover V8 engine, instead of a Jaguar one, wouldn't fit.

▼ With its raised roofline and myriad detail changes, the 1979 Series III XJ remains the only production Jaguar designed by an outside consultant.

than the iron-block XK. It appeared in an XJ-S Coupe, as well as a new two-seater Cabriolet with fixed side windows, a lift-out Targa-top roof and fold-down hood.

To put Jaguar back in the eye of the broader public, the XJ-S entered production-car racing in 1982 in partnership with Tom Walkinshaw Racing. It took such a good fight to

the dominating BMW 6-series that, in 1984, the team won the European Touring Car Championship.

Within four years customer satisfaction levels with Jaguars had soared, despite the core XJ saloon now being over 15 years old, and exports to the crucial North American market in particular were booming again. The British government decided it was time to cash in on Jaguar's rediscovered mojo and privatise the company. A stock-market flotation was organised in 1984, and it was a resounding success, with the share offer oversubscribed eight times.

Sir William Lyons died on 8 February 1985, a far happier man than he had been a decade before,

▲ XJ6 bodyshell manufacture at Castle Bromwich, where incoming boss John Egan oversaw huge quality jumps from 1980.

▲ Egan found a firm ally in Lyons as he turned Jaguar around. Here they are together in 1984 with Jaguars new and old.

because Jaguar was on top of its health declined,' recalled Michael game again.

'For a while, Grandpa was really quite depressed about what had happened to his company, and his

Quinn, his grandson and himself a Jaguar dealer for many years. He recalled the restorative effect of John Egan. 'Egan said: "We'd love to have you back as honorary Grandpa had been sneaking into president." Grandpa said: "Very kind Browns Lane almost weekly. He of you but, actually, I already am." could never totally let go.'

▼ The XJ-S HE was new for 1981 with a clever cylinder-head redesign that cut fuel thirst by a fifth, and new alloy wheels.

▲ Jaguar returned to racing, with help from TWR, and the XJS team swept the board of the European Touring Car Championship in 1984.

Egan and Lyons got on famously. 'He was a joy to work with,' Egan recalled. 'I could puzzle things out with Bill. I had a very rough relationship with the rest of BL, so it was nice to have someone like that who wasn't trying to kick me in the balls all the time!'

In 1986, Jaguar launched its all-new XJ, often known by its development codename of XJ40. Under the bonnet of the swish new saloon, whose styling was a modernisation of the original XJ6s, was the AJ6 engine in 2.9- and 3.6-litre forms. There was a new double-wishbone rear suspension, and a five-speed manual or four-speed automatic transmission choice. It had been a very long time coming;

▶ After a design process lasting thirteen strife-filled years, the new XJ6 – codenamed XJ40 – finally arrived in 1986.

▲ Full use was made of traditional leather and wood veneer for the neat and luxurious XJ40 interior, as customers demanded.

Bob Knight began designing the car thirteen years earlier. Egan described the development of the XJ40 and AJ6 engine as 'skunk work', done in spare moments when hard-pressed engineers weren't firefighting the XJ6 and XJ-S. 'I only had 200 engineers and I needed 1,200,' he recalled. Consequently, the XJ40 suffered some teething problems, especially in its none-too-dependable electrical department, and that was despite 5.5 million miles of prototype testing.

There was much to celebrate in June 1988, when Jaguar tasted victory once again at Le Mans. Tom Walkinshaw managed to break Porsche's stranglehold on the event when his purpose-built Group C XJR-9 car driven by Jan Lammers, Johnny Dumfries and Andy Wallace was first across the line at the 4 p.m. finish. It was the best way possible to signal that Jaguar was a force to be reckoned with.

► In 1993, a 6-litre V12 engine arrived, belatedly, in the XJ40-type cars; here the Jaguar XJ12 is in the foreground, its Daimler Double Six sister behind.

J aguar enjoyed less than six years as a truly independent company before the allure of its name and heritage proved irresistible to takeover. As the Ford then by someone else, was shares were openly traded on the London Stock Exchange, any company could mount a hostile bid, but the Ford Motor Company preferred to do it the gentlemanly way. It had already acquired Aston Martin in 1987; now, in October 1989, it tabled a full bid for Jaguar, but only if the board of the Coventry company agreed. In return, Ford promised to properly cherish the integrity of the Jaguar and Daimler marques, and keep Jaguar Cars a separate legal entity with its own board of directors.

In February 1990 the deal was completed, valuing Jaguar at £1.65 billion and pulling it into the Ford orbit. A takeover, if not by inevitable. Still, John Egan, who left six months later to be replaced by veteran Ford executive Bill Hayden, had his misgivings: 'I don't think they understood what to do with this company. But I knew that if I stayed I couldn't keep them off my back with the recession coming. There were hard times ahead, and they would seize complete control.'

A year later, by far the most expensive and startling Jaguar ever went on sale: the mid-engined XJ220 supercar. It began life at the 1988 Birmingham Motor Show as a concept car showpiece, with Jaguar's V12 engine mounted behind the two seats, and four-wheel drive. After three years incubation with Tom Walkinshaw's TWR Group, the production car was now ready for its strictly limited 350 potential customers. It was built in a new factory at Bloxham, near Oxford, part of the JaguarSport joint-venture between Walkinshaw and Jaguar. There were, however, a few significant changes from the show car: drive was to the rear wheels only, and the V12 engine was jettisoned for a twin-turbo 3.5-litre V6 that started life powering the MG Metro 6R4 rally car.

JAGUAR XJ220

On sale: 1992–94

Engine capacity, configuration: 3,498cc, V6

Body style: two-door, two-seater coupe

Dimensions: 4,860mm long, 1,150mm high, 2,000mm wide; wheelbase: 2,640mm

Top speed: 213mph

Acceleration: 0–60mph in 3.6sec.

Price: £403,000

▲ Left: Jaguar's XJ220 supercar was independently tested to reach 213mph, although it proved difficult to sell.

Right: TWR's XJR-9 sports-racer took Jaguar back to the Le Mans 24-hour race, which it won in 1988; cigarette sponsorship was entirely normal at the time ...

The only road test ever conducted on the XJ220 proved it had a phenomenal top speed of 213mph. Jaguar created the car to trounce supercar rivals like the Ferrari F40 and Porsche 959. The timing, however, proved inauspicious. By the time it was on sale, a deep economic recession had bitten hard; only 280 of the planned 350 cars were built, and the efforts buyers went to to wriggle free of their orders, forfeiting their deposits in the process, made national headlines.

Back in 1990, Jaguar contested the Daytona 24-hour endurance race in Florida with its new V12-powered XJR-12, and the cars

⌄ Left. June 1988 and Jan Lammers brings the TWR/ Jaguar Jaguar/Sport XJR-9 across the line to win the grueling Le Mans 24-hour epic. Right: the TWR-designed Jaguar XJR-14 had a lacklustre season in 1991, after which Jaguar withdrew from racing once again.

finished first and second. Then the team took four of them back to Le Mans, and the Brundle/Cobb/ Nielsen trio won, giving Jaguar its seventh victory there; the XJR-12 that came second helped fend off no fewer than nineteen Porsches. In 1991 the Le Mans achievement, although not an outright win, was still epic: the all-new XJR-14s came

second, third and fourth, reflecting Jaguar's near dominance of the World Sportscar Championship that year.

The first Jaguar wholly developed under Ford's watchful eye took its bow at the 1994 Paris Motor Show – the new X300 XJ saloon to replace the XJ40-type. Aside from the reinstated four round-headlamps

▲ Daimler (foreground) and Jaguar long-wheelbase versions of the new X300-type XJ range, introduced in 1994.

frontage for the whole range (many deplored the rectangular lamps of the XJ40), the most attention-grabbing aspect was the supercharged 4-litre AJ6 engine, a 326bhp motor with such storming performance that it could equal the V12 model (now a 6-litre) for its 155mph outright speed, and leave it trailing for acceleration. It was a first in a mass-produced saloon car, although a 3.2-litre six was also available.

These power units weren't offered for long. Ford investment had funded an all-new V8, the AJ-V8, designed and engineered at Jaguar and to be built at Ford's engine plant in Bridgend, South Wales. This hastened the closure of Jaguar's Radford, Coventry plant, an ex-Daimler facility it had used to manufacture engines and axles; it also meant goodbye to the awe-inspiring Jaguar V12 engine after

The Jaguar S-type used Ford's DEW98 platform, with independent double-wishbone suspension all round. Sharing a chassis structure was commonplace across the car industry by the 1990s, but few people realised the S-type was similar to the Lincoln LS and the Ford Thunderbird under the surface.

twenty-five years. So, the renamed XJ8 now received the new V8 engine in 3.2- and 4-litre forms in 1996, with a 4-litre supercharged edition too.

This 4-litre V8, with 290bhp, was at the heart of Jaguar's next new car: the XK8 coupe and convertible. Receiving a warm reception at its 1996 Geneva unveiling, it was a handsome, ingenious and comprehensive re-bodying of the long-serving XJS. Well-off, middle-aged Jaguar traditionalists felt instantly at home with the sleek style and the standard ZF five-speed automatic gearbox ... and the old XJS quirk of a handbrake between the driver's seat and door. A fully performance-orientated XKR supercharged model followed.

Jaguar was still a maker of prestigious, high-end cars, rendering it a niche player compared to other premium marques such as BMW and

▲ The XJ8 of 1996 sported Jaguar's brand-new V8 engine under is bonnet in 3.2- and 4-litre forms, and also came with supercharging.

▲ The AJ-V8 engine project was bankrolled by new owner Ford, and was manufactured in Ford's Bridgend plant.

➤ Left: inside the XJ8 there was nothing to upset the Jaguar traditionalist accustomed to burr walnut and soft leather.

Right: the XK8 in coupe and convertible forms arrived in 1996, with Jaguar's new V8 engine, to supplant the XJS.

Mercedes-Benz. Its owner Ford was naturally keen to exploit the Jaguar name it had paid so much to acquire.

Despite early assurances that Jaguar would retain its fiercely guarded purity, the Detroit giant – accustomed to punching out tin-cans-on-wheels by the million every year – baulked at the notion that a new, smaller, more

affordable Jaguar would be designed in Coventry from scratch.

For such an executive car to take on the dominant BMW 5 Series, Ford insisted Jaguar must share a basic structure with other models made by the company. Perhaps because of this, the Jaguar S-type of 1998 was a highly self-consciously retro-looking

JAGUAR S-TYPE R

On sale: 2002-07
Engine capacity, configuration:
4,196cc, V8
Body style: four-door,
five-seater saloon
Dimensions: 4,877mm long,
1,423mm high, 1,818mm wide;
wheelbase: 2,909mm
Top speed: 155mph (limited)
Acceleration: 0-60mph in 5.3sec.
Price: £49,995

saloon – styled by long-term Jaguar designer Geoff Lawson – that evoked its 1960s namesake with an upright grille, four bulging headlights and a gracefully tapered tail. Starting at £27,613, it was much more affordable than even the cheapest XJ, and the range would eventually include 2.5- and 3-litre versions of Jaguar's new AJ-V6, 4- and 4.2-litre AJ-V8s, plus a 4.2-litre supercharged S-type R, with a massive 400bhp that enabled the car to rocket from 0 to 60mph in 5.3sec. This car, limited to 155mph but said to be capable of 191mph, was Jaguar's first 'boy racer' machine, adopting yet more Ford practices and tearing up the old marque rulebook into ever-smaller pieces ...

➤ This Union Jack-bedecked XK8 was the automotive star of Mike Myers' 2002 movie *Austin Powers in Goldmember.*

JaguarSport, the TWR-Jaguar sports and race car joint-venture, created the mid-engined XJR-15 as a roadgoing version of the XJR-14 Le Mans car. It was also raced by wealthy privateers in its own series.

▲ The Jaguar S-type made its debut in 1998 as a new, more accessible alternative to the BMW 5 Series.

▶ The decidedly retro theme of the S-type is evident from the back as the tail treatment is gracefully tapered.

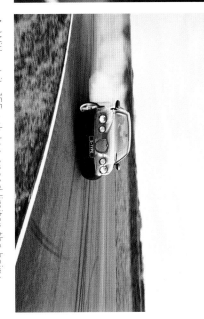

▶ Without its 155mph top-speed limiter, the hairy S-type R with 400bhp on tap was said to have been good for 191mph!

Given any other emblem on its prow, the X-type would have won fulsome praise from critics. But with the fangs of a leaping jaguar poking out of its radiator badge, expectations were naturally heightened.

The X-type was Jaguar's audacious move to target the BMW 3 Series, Lexus IS200 and Mercedes-Benz C-class head-on in the compact-executive car arena. Yet, to save costs in the fight with these purebreds, Ford insisted Jaguar adapt the platform of the Ford Mondeo to its needs. In fact, the whole concept was imposed on Jaguar by Ford's US bosses, including an insistence that a squashed-up rendition of the usually flowing Jaguar 'line' was what the market wanted.

To set the car apart, all models at its 2001 launch featured four-wheel drive, with torque split 40/60 between the front and back wheels. Lavish standard kit included leather upholstery, wood veneer trim, climate control, alloy wheels and an electric glass sunroof.

To make the car, Ford found space at its Halewood factory in Merseyside, once home to the Ford Escort, alongside the Land Rover Freelander. The aim was high volume, with aspirations to make 100,000 X-types a year to sell all over the world. It was a very good car to drive and own but not a game-changer, and sales never reached more than 50,000 annually. In 2004, a smart estate model – the first ever from Jaguar – was added and went down well, but later front-drive-only X-types with rather gutless 2.1-litre V6 petrol engines tended to reinforce the impression that the X-type, albeit entirely competent, was in no way special enough to carry the Jaguar name. In 2003 came a diesel X-type, another debatable first for Jaguar. The X-type was quietly axed in 2009.

The X-type estate, or 'Sportwagon' as it was named for the US market, was the first Jaguar styled by Ian Callum, who joined the company in 1999 after receiving much acclaim

for the Aston Martin DB7. His strong views on how Jaguars should look and the image they should convey (as a teenager he'd even sent his own Jaguar designs in to William Heynes and received sage career advice by return) started to elevate Jaguar's design activity from the commodity-driven restraints that epitomised the Ford approach.

His arrival was too late to influence the all-new XJ, codenamed X350, which enjoyed a muted 2003 launch. Here was a highly significant new luxury car, the first-ever built around an all-aluminium monocoque chassis that employed the world's first industrial rivet-bonded joining technology, with self-pierce rivets and epoxy adhesive joining together

By 2005, Jaguar had bowed to the industry norm and offered diesel-engine options in the X-type, S-type and XJ. To salute this, design head Ian Callum created the R-D6 concept car in 2003, a striking five-door hatchback with rear-hinged back doors and a 2.7-litre V6 diesel engine.

▼ At its launch, all X-types offered four-wheel drive, with the torque-split slightly biased towards the rear wheels.

▼ Shrinking traditional Jaguar lines around the chassis unit of the Ford Mondeo produced the controversial X-type of 2001.

➤ Jaguar finally gained its first estate car in the X-type, introduced in 2004.

▼ The R1 was the car that took Jaguar into its short and inglorious adventure in Formula 1.

pressings, castings and extrusions. But the look both outside and in the sumptuously appointed cabin was very old-school 'Jag', strongly redolent of the XJ6 that was first seen thirty-five years before. *Top Gear* magazine summed up the twenty-first-century problem: 'The current XJ is a world-beater wrapped in a very old-fashioned body that doesn't appeal to where America is right now. It has not one square centimetre of "bling".'

The remaining link to the Jaguar Cars organisation that William Lyons himself knew was severed in 2005. Carmaking at Browns Lane ended (the historic factory was soon bull-dozed) as the entire manufacture of the XJ shifted to the Castle

▲ For the next-generation XJ of 2003, codenamed X350, Jaguar moved to an all-aluminium body structure.

▶ The 2003 XJ had an olde-worlde elegance that, sadly, was a little out of step with the contemporary demands for 'bling'.

Bromwich plant near Birmingham, there as well. Ford had systemati-The last XK8, with vestiges of the cally dismantled Jaguar's in-house Lyons' influenced XJS, was built expertise in making things like seats and dashboards, buying them in from outside suppliers instead. A firm that had once been home to armies of Jaguar craftsmen, all half-moon glasses and pencils behind ears, became an assembly operation where cars were bolted together.

And yet ... this is where wistfulness about Jaguar's glory days ended and the possibilities of the future began.

For one thing, there was an environmental upside to the streamlining. In 2003, painted bodies for 27,000 XJ saloons and 6,000 XK coupes had to be carted, eight per transporter, the 12 miles from Castle Bromwich to assembly at Browns Lane. All these truck movements, and the associated pollution, were eliminated.

Then Ian Callum's Advanced Lightweight Coupe concept car, revealed in 2004, became a very close rendition of the all-new XK that went on sale two years later. The gorgeous-looking GT and con-vertible were instantly desirable and as technically interesting as they were shimmeringly attractive; the Castle Bromwich-made duo adopt-ed the XJ's all-alloy construction, and also pushed pedestrian safety standards forward with the innova-tion of a Pyrotechnic Pedestrian Deployable Bonnet System, coor-dinated to reduce the severity of pedestrian injuries by 'popping up' to cushion the blow of any impact.

Much more commercially important was the new mid-range

Clockwise from top left: the brand new XK coupe and convertible of 2006 put Jaguar triumphantly back on the map for sporting desirability; the XK convertible could be had with V6 or V8 engines and was an immediate hit with critics and customers; the first XK rolls off the production line at Castle Bromwich, the former body plant that now builds the whole car.

XF saloon, which arrived in 2007. As Jaguar's most mainstream model, it was forced to stick to an updated version of the platform of the S-type it replaced, but the all-new body, with an especially bold grille treatment and a new dynamism to its side profile, was Ian Callum's most profound, real-life design statement yet about 'new Jaguar'. Inside, the luxury cabin featured a unique, pop-up rotary gear selector for the six-speed (later eight-speed) gearbox. Over its nine-year lifetime, more than 200,000 first-generation examples were sold, including models specially tailored for police use.

A couple of years later came the all-new XJ luxury saloon, an even more dramatic car with its radical 'cat's claws' rear lights and a full-length glass sunroof. There was a choice of 5-litre V8 engines with or without supercharging, 3-litre V6s in supercharged petrol or twin-turbo diesel forms, and two- or four-wheel drive. By 2010, British Prime Minister David Cameron was seen regularly at home and around the world using one (with armour plating and an emergency oxygen supply) as his official transport.

As is doubtless evident by the chronology of this book, the motor industry – despite the multi-billion-pound finance, canny decision-making and many years of development time needed to bring future models to customers – is subject to frequent, and sudden changes in strategy. Throughout the 1990s Ford had been acquiring prestige brands: in 1999 it gathered these into its Premier Automotive Group, with headquarters in London.

By 2007, though, it changed its mind, opting to concentrate on Ford, and to offload its other brands. In 2008 it announced it would sell both Jaguar and Land Rover to the Tata conglomerate. They were immediately brought together in Tata's new Jaguar Land Rover (JLR) subsidiary. The company became Indian-owned but was now given the freedom to forge its own distinctive path. With its three large manufacturing facilities at Castle Bromwich, Solihull and Halewood; its two design centres at Gaydon, Warwickshire and Whitley, Coventry; and two of the greatest marque names in the whole of motoring history, things were getting exciting.

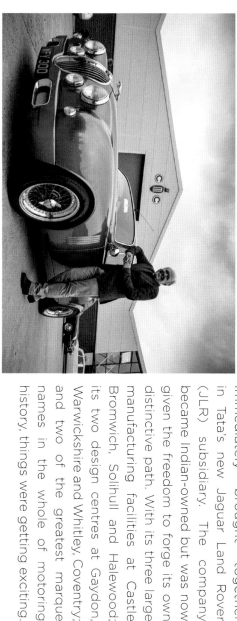

▼ Jaguar design chief Ian Callum with his personal Jaguar Mk2: the subject of some radical customisation.

▲ 'Cat's claw' rear lights were a highly distinctive aspect of the new, aluminium-made XJ.

◄ The XF of 2007 was a true turnaround car for Jaguar, replacing the S-type and selling more than 200,000 examples.

Jaguar offered a Daimler edition of the XJ almost constantly until 2008, the final one named the Daimler Super Eight and based on the X350. After that, Jaguar agreed not to use the brand any longer, allowing the holding company for Mercedes-Benz to adopt the worldwide title of Daimler AG.

10 JAGUAR LAND ROVER, MAKING BRITISH CARS GREAT AGAIN

The first day of January 2013 brought an important turning point for Jaguar. It was the day when Jaguar Cars Limited and Land Rover were brought together as one operating company and renamed Jaguar Land Rover Automotive PLC. Although still owned outright by India's Tata Motors, this was a clear statement that Britain's most famous sports and luxury car marque really was now fully integrated with its world-famous four-wheel-drive vehicle brand. That year, the man in overall charge of this prestigious entity, chief executive Dr Ralf Speth, revealed the company as the most significant investor in research and development in the British motor

industry, with £3 billion poured into an avalanche of new products. The year before, Jaguar had already added a versatile estate car iteration of the XF to its line-up. But in 2013 the results of the R&D mega-splurge began to show with the launch of the F-type, a two-seater sports car that represented the long-overdue spiritual successor to the E-type (an earlier 'F-type', also known as XJ41, had been designed in the Egan era but was cancelled after the Ford takeover).

The muscular-looking roadster, with a coupe to follow in 2014, rode on a shortened version of the XK's all-aluminium platform, and was strictly a two-seater. It came with a choice of 3-litre V6 and fierce 5-litre V8 supercharged engines, and the 587bhp F-type SVR unleashed in 2016 was the first Jaguar since the controversial XJ220 able to kiss 200mph.

A premium carmaker that doesn't produce its own engines is an anomaly, and Ford had cut this aspect from Jaguar's activities by shifting engine-making to its Bridgend plant. In 2011, Jaguar Land Rover set out to reassert its motor-making skills by sinking £355m into a brand-new factory at the i54 business park in Wolverhampton, where it would manufacture a brand-new family of economical four-cylinder petrol and diesel engines for Jaguars and Land Rovers. It was officially opened on 30 October 2014 by Her Majesty

▼ Jaguar Land Rover was formed in 2008 after Ratan Tata (third from right) acquired both marques and brought in Ralf Speth (second from left) to run the new company.

JAGUAR F-TYPE 3.0

On sale: 2014-now
Engine capacity, configuration: 2,995cc, V6
Body style: two-door, two-seater convertible
Dimensions: 4,470cc long, 1,308mm high, 2,042mm wide; wheelbase: 2,622mm
Top speed: 161mph
Acceleration: 0–60mph in 5.5sec.
Price: £57,880

▼ The spiritual successor to the Jaguar E-type finally arrived in 2014 as the F-type, the company's first genuine sports car in almost forty years.

The Queen. Not long afterwards, the company said it was swelling its workforce at the Land Rover plant in Solihull by a quarter, creating 1,000 extra jobs.

The reason for all this expansion was revealed in 2014 in the shape of the new Jaguar XE, a compact sports saloon that would fill the role of the late and unlamented X-type. With the chassis, body and easily tuned wishbone/multi-link suspension (the rear system was subframe-mounted) all made from aluminium, here was the first car from the company to use a new modular platform structure, and it was engineered for both rear- and four-wheel drive, an indication that the same hardware would underpin Land Rovers to come. To give the car perfect 50-50 balance between front and rear, the battery was in the boot, and the boot floor itself was in weightier steel. All clever stuff that helped the still relatively small JLR square up to the giants of German premium car-making.

▶ Left: the XE was the first compact Jaguar sports saloon since the X-type, and enjoyed major and immediate success.

Right: Jaguar entered the sport-utility vehicle arena with the F-Pace, here giving a two-wheel demonstration of its roadholding at Goodwood.

The XE was to be built at Solihull on the same line as the Range Rover Sport. It was the first conventional saloon to emerge from there since the Rover SD1 of 1977, and the first to use the new 2-litre Ingenium engines from the Wolverhampton factory. This British alternative to a BMW 3 Series received rave reviews when it went on sale in 2015, and could boast exceptional aerodynamics, with a drag co-efficient of just 0.26. Huge demand saw a second production line open at Castle Bromwich, and the whole of XE manufacture decamped there in 2016. This was to free up space at Solihull for Jaguar's next new model,

▶ Jaguar was late to the SUV market with its F-Pace – BMW had launched its X5 some twenty years previously.

In the second decade of the twenty-first century, Jaguar went multi-national. An assembly plant for the XF and XJ opened in Pune, India, in 2011; a joint venture with China's Chery saw the XE and XF enter production in Changsu in 2014, with Ingenium engines added locally in 2017; and a JLR plant opened in Nitra, Slovakia, in 2018.

the F-Pace sport-utility vehicle, truly its first, the X5, back in 1997). It was more evidence that sharing components with Land Rover was a a departure for the marque after so many years shunning the sector (BMW, for instance, introduced valuable key to extending Jaguar into new areas.

The closeness intensified yet further in 2017 with the launch of the E-Pace, Jaguar's first compact SUV. There simply was no room at any JLR UK assembly plant to accommodate this potentially high-volume car, and so manufacture was farmed out to contractor Magna Steyr in Graz, Austria.

The marque made its first and so far only foray into Formula 1 in 2000, effectively rebranding the Stewart F1 team. It wasn't exactly successful, the best result that could be achieved was two third places for

Eddie Irvine in the 2001 Monaco and 2002 Italian Grands Prix.

This misadventure ended in 2004, but Jaguar was back on the grid in 2016 as a participant in the all-electric Formula E series, and some of what it learnt from this green motor sport experience found a home in the i-Pace, the all-electric spin-off from the E-Pace, with its two electric motors providing all-wheel drive and a claimed range of 290 miles on a full charge of its innovative lithium-ion battery. The Ian Callum-designed car was described as a 'five-seater sports car' and was also built in Austria with the E-Pace.

The recent desire to have a brand-new Jaguar on the drive has seen sales snowball. In 2013, 58,593 cars were sold; by 2017, that had all but trebled to 172,848. Enthusiasts who have stuck with Jaguar through thick and thin should feel proud that it's as relevant and desirable today as the first sidecar was to William Lyons back in 1922.

➤ Jaguar's entry in the single-seater, all-electric Formula E race series has helped put it at the forefront of alternative-fuel high-performance cars.

➤ The E-Pace brings Jaguar into the 'crossover' SUV market with its new Ingenium four-cylinder engines, producing spectacular results.

➤ I-Pace is an all-electric compact car from Jaguar, as the marque heads into the evolving future of the automobile.

JAGUAR I-PACE

On sale: 2018–now

Engine capacity, configuration: twin electric motors, 90kWh lithium-ion battery

Body style: four-door, five-seater SUV

Dimensions: 4,682mm long, 1,565mm high, 2,011mm wide; wheelbase: 2,990mm

Top speed: 124mph

Acceleration: 0–60mph in 4.5sec.

Price: £63,495